WHERE'S WALLY?

Based on the
characters created by
MARTIN HANDFORD

THE
TRULY
TERRIFIC

ACTIVITY
BOOK

WALKER BOOKS

AND SUBSIDIARIES

LONDON • BOSTON • SYDNEY

DEEP SEA DIVERS

WELCOME, WALLY WATCHERS, TO WALLY AND WENDA'S WATERY WORLD! HERE WE ARE IN THE LAND OF THE DEEP SEA DIVERS. EVERYTHING IS GETTING BACK TO NORMAL NOW THAT PEGBEARD'S PIRATE SHIP HAS SUNK. THERE IS LOTS OF TREASURE TO BE FOUND BUT WE ARE LOOKING FOR ONE PIECE IN PARTICULAR. HERE'S YOUR CLUE:

LUCINDA THE MERMAID IS WAVING AT YOU. FIND HER A JEWEL THAT'S PRECIOUS AND BLUE.

THINGS TO DO

Here are the outlines of some islands and their names. To make life really hard for you, we've mixed up all the letters in the names. Can you untangle them?

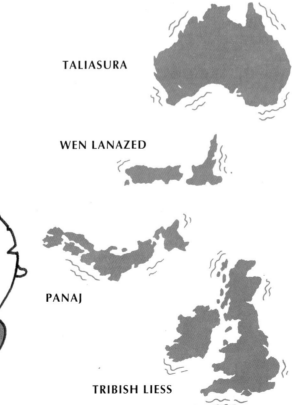

TALIASURA

WEN LANAZED

PANAJ

TRIBISH LIESS

DID YOU KNOW?

The aqualung, a tank containing compressed air, was first developed by Jacques Cousteau and Emile Gagnan for underwater exploration in 1943.

High divers from La Quebrada in Acapulco, Mexico, dive from cliffs which are 26½ metres high into water which is only 3½ metres deep. Wow!

In 1989 Angela Bandini of Italy held her breath for 2 minutes and 46 seconds while diving down to 107 metres. An extremely dangerous thing to do!

The Lutine bell, which was salvaged from a wrecked British warship, hangs in the insurance office of Lloyds of London in England. It is rung every time a ship is reported missing or destroyed at sea.

MUSHROOM-MINING TROLLS

WOW! THERE'S NOTHING
LIKE HAVING SOME FUN
WHILE YOU DIG, AND THE
MUSHROOM-MINING TROLLS
CERTAINLY KNOW ALL
ABOUT HAVING FUN. THE
MAIN MUSHROOM-MINING TROLL,
WHO IS WEARING A MEDAL, IS NOT
AS HAPPY AS HE COULD BE:

WE HAVE FUN AT WORK,
THAT IS PLAIN TO SEE.
BUT WHO'S TAKEN MY YO-YO?
WHERE CAN IT BE?

WHO TOOK IT? CAN YOU SPOT HIM?
AND WHICH TROLL IS MISSING
A LIGHT BULB FROM HIS HAT?
MEANWHILE, I MUST START LOOKING
FOR WOOF. I KNOW HE'S AROUND
HERE SOMEWHERE.

THINGS TO DO

Can you help Trumpeter Troll collect 10 musical notes and then join the other members of the band?

DID YOU KNOW?

Mushrooms and toadstools belong to the huge fungi family, which has more than 100,000 different types of fungi in it!

Unlike our happy Mushroom Miners, trolls in old Scandinavian stories are horrible forest dwellers with magical powers. They aren't very bright, so they are often outwitted.

A mycologist is a person who studies fungi.

WHAT FABULOUS FLYING FUN IN THE PERSIAN CARPET BAZAAR! EVEN WHITEBEARD AND WOOF HAVE JOINED IN. ALI BLOBI'S HENCHMEN ARE LOOKING FOR ALI'S CARPET, WHICH FLEW AWAY BECAUSE HE TREATED IT SO BADLY – HE NEVER HOOVERED IT! CRUMBS! WELL, HERE'S A CLUE TO HELP YOU SPOT THIS MESSY MAT:

THIS RUG'S ON THE RUN FROM A DIRTY OLD STINKER. IT'S BEEN CAUGHT BY A LADY HOOK, LINE AND SINKER!

THERE ARE TWO TIMEPIECES IN THE PICTURE, TELLING US THAT TIME IS RUNNING OUT. CAN YOU SPOT THEM IN THIS RUG RUSH?

FLYING CARPETS

DID YOU KNOW?

Persian carpets, unlike ordinary carpets, are not woven. They are knotted together by hand.

In ancient Persia, walnuts were once so rare that they were used as money.

The Metropolitan Museum in New York paid one million dollars for a Persian carpet made in 1590. This is the highest price ever paid for a carpet.

The Persians were the first people to give each other birthday cakes.

THINGS TO DO

Here are 6 heads of Ali Blobi. Only 2 are identical.
Can you tell which they are?

a

b

c

d

e

f

DUNGEONS

DID YOU KNOW?

Alcatraz means "pelican" in Spanish. The old prison in San Francisco Bay, USA, is called Alcatraz because of the pelicans which fly around it.

In the eighteenth and nineteenth centuries, old galleons were used as floating prisons. These were called hulks.

One of the most famous prisoners ever was Napoleon Bonaparte. He was imprisoned on the island of Elba in 1814, but escaped after 100 days. After the battle of Waterloo he was sent to another island, St Helena, where he eventually died.

A palindrome is a word or sentence which reads the same backwards or forwards.
Napoleon is supposed to have said: *"Able was I ere I saw Elba."*

Another palindrome is: *"Madam, I'm Adam."*

Can you think of any?

THINGS TO DO

WANTED
ODLAW'S HEROES

a FLASH

b BONO

c THE KID

d JAKE
5

Here are portraits of some of my favourite chaps. Each one has stolen something from the picture opposite. Tee hee, my heroes! Can you spot what they've pinched?

HI THERE!
ODLAW, ARCH-VILLAIN AND THOROUGHLY NASTY CHAP, AT YOUR SERVICE. IF YOU THINK I HAVE COME HERE TO VISIT SOME FRIENDS THEN YOU REALLY DON'T KNOW ME VERY WELL! I'M LOOKING FOR SOMETHING WHICH I'VE BEEN TOLD WILL MAKE ME INCREDIBLY RICH. ALL I HAVE TO GO ON IS THIS RIDDLE:

WORSHIPPED IN EGYPT
WITH NINE LIVES TO BOOT.
I STAND SHAPED IN GOLD
NEAR A STRIPED BATHING SUIT.

IF YOU CAN HELP ME I PROMISE TO GIVE YOU A HUGE PRIZE. ODLAW NEVER GOES BACK ON HIS PROMISE – WELL, NOT SINCE YESTERDAY! ENOUGH TALK.
GET SEARCHING!

UNDERGROUND HUNTERS

WE'VE JUST TUNNELLED OUR WAY DOWN TO THE DEPTHS TO VISIT THE UNDERGROUND HUNTERS. THEY ARE HERE FOR A VERY SPECIAL OCCASION. TODAY IS THE WEDDING OF SAMMY SNAKE AND SYLVIE SERPENT. I AM SURE YOU CAN SPOT THEM EASILY! BUT CAN YOU SEE SLIPPERY SID THE SLIMY? HE IS ALSO AFTER SYLVIE'S AFFECTIONS AND HAS GATE-CRASHED THE PARTY. HERE'S A CLUE TO HELP YOU FIND HIM:

SID LONGS FOR SYLVIE WITHOUT ANY TIES! STRANGE THAT HE CHOSE ONE AS HIS DISGUISE!

WHILE HUNTING, LOOK FOR SOME OF THEIR WEDDING PRESENTS: A FISH OUT OF WATER, A COMB AND A WATCH.

GOOD LUCK!

THINGS TO DO

Look at this mass of snakes and see if you can find which one is coming out of the basket.

DID YOU KNOW?

A fossil of a python 38 million years old was found in Egypt. When it was alive and slithering across the sands, it must have been over 11 metres long.

An 8 metre anaconda has been known to swallow a 45 kilo pig whole! Wow!

There are 3 types of cobra which, instead of injecting poison into their victims with a bite, spray venom into their eyes!

2800 different species of snake live on Earth.

A rattlesnake's rattle begins to grow at birth. Each time the snake sheds its skin, a new hard tip is formed at the end of the tail. The tip from the old skin remains and these gradually build up into a series of hard, hollow shells which rattle when the snake moves its tail.

1   2   3

STONE AGE

FANTASTIC!

HERE'S YOUR TYPICAL STONE AGE SUNDAY MORNING. EVERYONE IS HAVING A ROLLICKING, ROCKING GOOD TIME, ESPECIALLY ROCKSY – CARN'S GUITAR PLAYING HAS BOULDER OVER (HA HA!). CAN YOU HELP THE CHIEF MUSHROOM-MINING TROLL FIND THE MISSING INGREDIENT HE NEEDS FOR HIS HUNGRY HISTORY HASH RECIPE? HERE'S A CLUE:

A TOADSTOOL THAT'S PERFECT FOR FOUL WITCHES' BREW, GROWING OVER YOUR HEAD COLOURED YELLOW AND BLUE.

I'VE A FEELING IT'S ONLY A STONE'S THROW AWAY...

GOOD LUCK.

DID YOU KNOW?

The earliest cave paintings are 30,000 years old. They were discovered in 1875.

The person who discovered the first cave paintings, in Spain, was thought to have forged them. It was not until others were found in France that his name was cleared.

A favourite subject for cave paintings was hunting. Stone Age Man sometimes signed his pictures by blowing pigment around his hand, leaving a hand print on the cave wall.

The most famous cave paintings were found in Lascaux in France in 1940.

THINGS TO DO

Hidden in this wordsearch are the words for 10 things in the picture. Can you find them?

```
K I V O A L H G W L B
T M R E S P E A R A L
R M A M M O T H S D Y
S Y S T A S V Z J D W
K A U R H T C H R E X
I J I B R M E I F R Q
T P T O B A B Y D P L
E I C L F N T E A H A
A R A W G I E R M W D
L F S Z A T H N O G D
B R E M A M M H R L E
O B R I D G E D B E L
```

THE GREAT BALL GAME

WORKING OUT THE RULES OF THE GREAT BALL GAME IS ALWAYS A LOT OF FUN, O FANATICAL FANS OF WALLY. BUT YOU MUST REMEMBER TWO THINGS – THE RULES CHANGE EVERY FEW MINUTES AND SOMETIMES THERE ARE NO RULES AT ALL! SEE IF YOU CAN SPOT THE CAPTAINS OF THE TWO TEAMS WITH THE HELP OF THIS CLUE:

CAPTAIN BART
HAS A BROKEN HEART,
CAPTAIN LOU
HIDES A BALL FROM YOU.

TO WORK OUT THE SCORE, COUNT ALL THE ORANGE BALLS FOR BART'S TEAM AND ALL THE PLAYERS WITH GREEN UNIFORMS FOR LOU'S. WHICH TEAM IS WINNING?

THINGS TO DO

Here's a drawing of a special sportsman. How many sports do you think he can play?

DID YOU KNOW?

The oldest set of marbles ever found was in the grave of an Egyptian child dated 3000 BC. The marbles were rounded, semi-precious stones.

A game called "Tsu Chu", which means "to kick a ball of stuffed leather", was played in China more than 2500 years ago.

A game very similar to basketball called "Pok-ta-Pok" was played in the tenth century BC by the Olmecs in Mexico.

The first ever winner of an Olympic event was Coroibos, a cook, who won a foot race in 776 BC.

VIKINGS

DID YOU KNOW?

The Vikings founded many cities throughout Europe and the Far East, including Dublin, the capital city of the Republic of Ireland.

The word "Vikings" means pirates!

Leif Eriksson, the Viking, landed in North America and established a colony there called Vinland, 500 years before Columbus.

Viking boats were called "Long Ships" and could be over 24 metres in length.

Only some Vikings were pirates. Most were wonderfully efficient farmers.

A tax called the Danegeld was levied in England to pay the Vikings so that they would not invade.

Unlike the characters in our picture, the real Vikings never had horns on their helmets.

THINGS TO DO

Look carefully at these shadows and see if you can match them to the people and objects in the picture. But be careful. One of them is back to front!

AZTECS

DID YOU KNOW?

The Aztecs' capital was called Tenochtitlan and was built in the marshes of Lake Tezcuco. This is now the site of Mexico City.

The Aztecs were only one of 3 civilizations living in Mexico between 900 and 1500 AD. The others were the Mayans and the Toltecs.

The Aztecs never used iron, not even for tools or weapons. They didn't have the wheel either.

The Aztecs took their ball games seriously. Sometimes the captain of the losing team would have his head cut off!

There were about 5 million Aztecs in 1519 when the conquest by the Spanish began.

THINGS TO DO

This Aztec temple has been damaged in a terrible earthquake. Can you count how many stone blocks the Aztecs will need to repair it?

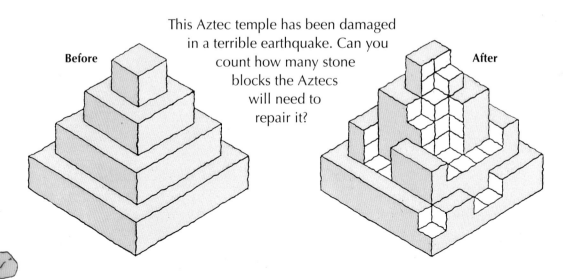

Before

After

WELL, WORLD-WIDE FOLLOWERS OF WALLY, AS YOU CAN SEE, WENDA AND I HAVE BEEN HERE BEFORE. WE LEFT BEHIND A PAIR OF GLASSES, AN UMBRELLA AND ONE OF OUR HATS. LOOK FOR THEM, BUT FIRST WARN THE AZTECS OF APPROACHING DANGER. HERE'S A CLUE:

THERE'S A SPY IN THE VILLAGE, IN DISGUISE IT IS SAID. HE HAS NOT GOT A HELMET BUT A FLAG ON HIS HEAD!

SPOT THE SPY AND THE HELMET HE USUALLY WEARS. CAN YOU GUESS WHY THE AZTECS ARE IN DANGER? THE FACTS ON THIS PAGE WILL HELP YOU. THE MASKED PHANTOM AVENGER MAY BE ABLE TO SAVE THE AZTECS. SPOT HIM TOO.

SPACE MUSEUM

JEEPERS, CREEPERS, LOOK AT ALL THESE PEEPERS! NOBODY SEEMS TOO WORRIED BY A COUPLE OF INTER-GALACTIC GATE- OR SHOULD I SAY, WALL-CRASHERS. WELL, THE WACKIEST MUSEUM IN THE UNIVERSE CERTAINLY GIVES VALUE FOR MONEY. SPEAKING OF WHICH, SOMEONE HAS THEIR EYES ON TODAY'S TAKINGS. SEE IF YOU CAN TELL WHO, FROM THIS CLUE, OH INTREPID INVESTIGATORS:

HE HAS THE KEY
TO THE PERFECT CRIME.
A STRIPY BOX
IS HIS AIM THIS TIME!

HE'S GOING TO HAVE QUITE A JOB TRYING TO HIDE FROM ALL OF THOSE EYES!

DID YOU KNOW?

The word "robot" was first used in a play called *R.U.R.* written in 1921 by Karel Capek.

The Volkswagen Beetle or Bug sold more than any other car. Its appearance has changed very little since 1934 when it was first designed.

Washing machines were first sold in 1832, but the first electrically-powered machines did not appear until 1914.

The movie which has made the most money ever is *E.T.* which has grossed over $700 million!

Two other movies based on space travel are among the most popular films ever made: *Star Wars* and *Close Encounters of the Third Kind.*

THINGS TO DO

Try saying these tongue twisters as fast as you can:

Seventy-six saucy spaceships soar the southern solar system!

Modern Martians must admire a moving masterpiece apiece!

Crashing crafts of cretinous cryptons career carelessly.

The Many Moons Museum makes many a minute's magical musing!

Can you untwist these words which have become mixed up in the madcap museum mayhem! They should each spell the name of a planet in our solar system:

TOPUL

ASTURN

RETIPUJ

CURRYME

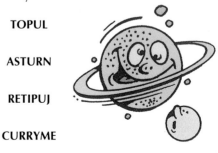

CHECK LIST

FLYING CARPETS

- A man reading a book
- A carpet with a hole in it
- A man rolled in a carpet
- A man wearing a scarf
- An hour glass
- An urn with stars
- An alarm clock
- A crashed carpet
- A lady sleeping
- 2 men arguing
- A telescope
- A skateboard
- A golf club

DUNGEON

- 2 mousetraps
- A television set
- A fork and spoon
- A blindfolded prisoner
- A balloon and chain
- A squirting fish
- A fizzy drink
- A maid
- A basketball
- A painting
- A beard in irons
- A waiter

DEEP SEA DIVERS

- 2 dancing fish
- 2 flying fish
- A heart
- A swordfish
- A sawfish
- 4 diving helmets
- A golden anchor
- 2 fish playing cards
- A climbing eel
- A boot
- A fork and spoon
- A ruby ring
- A pirate octopus
- A polka dot starfish
- A salt shaker
- A periscope

TROLLS

- A biplane
- A motor car
- A wristwatch
- A flying saucer
- A troll trapped in a zipper
- A magnifying glass
- 2 trolls wearing mushrooms
- A cassette tape
- A striped bucket
- A lighted match
- A jack-in-the-mushroom
- 2 chicken drumsticks
- A bow-and-mushroom
- 3 fizzy drinks

UNDERGROUND HUNTERS

- A snake in a bottle
- A bookworm
- 2 snakes on the telephone
- A yo-yo
- 2 dragons
- A snake in a turban
- A tightrope walker
- A snaky spear
- 2 green matches
- A snake wearing lipstick
- 4 pairs of eyes
- 4 musical instruments
- A snake golf club

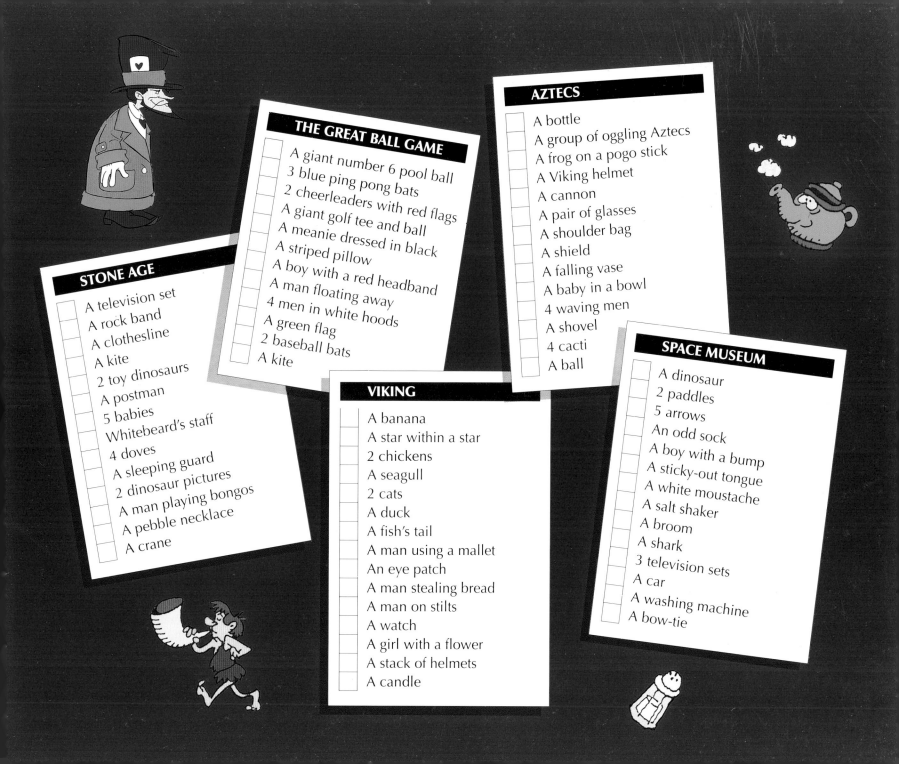

THE GREAT BALL GAME

- A giant number 6 pool ball
- 3 blue ping pong bats
- 2 cheerleaders with red flags
- A giant golf tee and ball
- A meanie dressed in black
- A striped pillow
- A boy with a red headband
- A man floating away
- 4 men in white hoods
- A green flag
- 2 baseball bats
- A kite

AZTECS

- A bottle
- A group of oggling Aztecs
- A frog on a pogo stick
- A Viking helmet
- A cannon
- A pair of glasses
- A shoulder bag
- A shield
- A falling vase
- A baby in a bowl
- 4 waving men
- A shovel
- 4 cacti
- A ball

STONE AGE

- A television set
- A rock band
- A clothesline
- A kite
- 2 toy dinosaurs
- A postman
- 5 babies
- Whitebeard's staff
- 4 doves
- A sleeping guard
- 2 dinosaur pictures
- A man playing bongos
- A pebble necklace
- A crane

VIKING

- A banana
- A star within a star
- 2 chickens
- A seagull
- 2 cats
- A duck
- A fish's tail
- A man using a mallet
- An eye patch
- A man stealing bread
- A man on stilts
- A watch
- A girl with a flower
- A stack of helmets
- A candle

SPACE MUSEUM

- A dinosaur
- 2 paddles
- 5 arrows
- An odd sock
- A boy with a bump
- A sticky-out tongue
- A white moustache
- A salt shaker
- A broom
- A shark
- 3 television sets
- A car
- A washing machine
- A bow-tie

ANSWERS

DEEP SEA DIVERS

Riddle: The blue gemstone is in the treasure chest in the bottom left-hand corner of the picture.
The islands are AUSTRALIA, NEW ZEALAND, JAPAN and the BRITISH ISLES.

MUSHROOM-MINING TROLLS

Riddle: The yo-yo has been taken by the troll in the top right-hand corner of the picture.
The troll who is missing a light bulb from his hat has a match instead. He's on the left of the picture, in the middle.
Woof is in the top left-hand corner.

FLYING CARPETS

Riddle: The messy mat is the blue one with a yellow fringe which has been caught by a fishing line. It is at the top of the picture near the middle.
The 2 time pieces are an alarm clock and an hour glass.
The 2 identical heads of Blobi are: a and d.

DUNGEONS

Riddle: Odlaw is looking for the gold cat on the right of the picture.
Odlaw's outlaws have stolen:
a = a duck; b = a pipe;
c = a fizzy drink; d = a running vest.

UNDERGROUND HUNTERS

Riddle: Slippery Sid the Slimy is the green and red striped snake being worn as a tie in the bottom left-hand corner of the picture.

Wedding presents: the fish out of water is at the top of the picture on the right; the comb is being waved by a red and white striped snake near the middle of the picture; the watch is being worn by an orange snake on the right-hand side of the picture.
Mass of snakes: 2.

STONE AGE

Riddle: The Chief Mushroom-Mining Troll is searching for a mushroom growing on the roof of a house near the centre of the picture.
Wordsearch

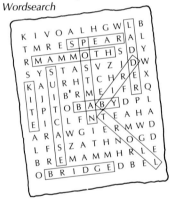

THE GREAT BALL GAME

Riddle: Captain Bart (wearing orange) is playing cards. He's in the bottom half of the picture, near the middle. Captain Lou (wearing green) has a ball inside his hat. He is standing behind Captain Bart.
The score is Lou's Shorts 7; Bart's Hoods 4.
The special sportsman can play 11 sports: ping pong; American football; cards; boxing; baseball; basketball; cricket; javelin; hockey; golf; scuba diving.

VIKINGS

Riddle: It's a golden apple painted black with the number "8" on it. The apple is in a box at the bottom of the picture near the middle.
Lars is in a barrel to the the left of the bananas.

AZTECS

The glasses are on the first step of the Aztec temple on the left of the picture. The umbrella is on the second step. The hat is on the thatched roof of the hut in the middle.
Riddle: The spy is on the top of the Aztec temple. He usually wears a helmet which is on the second step of the temple, near the umbrella. The Aztecs are in danger of attack by the Spanish. The masked avenger is in the bottom left-hand corner of the picture.
Aztec temple: 21 blocks are needed to repair it.

SPACE MUSEUM

Riddle: The intergalactic wall-crasher wearing a stripy shirt in the bottom left-hand corner of the picture has his eye on today's takings. They are in the stripy box at the bottom of the picture near the middle.
The scrambled planets are Pluto, Saturn, Jupiter and Mercury.

MORE THINGS TO DO

The fun's not over yet, Wally watchers! Have a look at the back cover. Each of the characters there appears at least once in our book. Can you spot them all, and find 13 scrolls?

The "creature" below is made up of one element from each of the large pictures in this book. Can you find which picture each piece comes from?

Happy hunting!

First published 1993 by Walker Books Ltd
87 Vauxhall Walk, London SE11 5HJ

8 9 10

Text © 1993 Martin Handford

The right of Martin Handford to be identified as author of this work has been asserted by him in accordance with the Copyright, Designs and Patents Act 1988.

This book has been typeset in Optima.

Printed in Great Britain

British Library Cataloguing in Publication Data A catalogue record for this book is available from the British Library.

ISBN 0-7445-3240-X